Nine Valiant Academicals

To Lawrence
with best wishes

Nine Valiant Academicals

Edinburgh Academical
holders of the Victoria Cross

Alasdair Macintyre

Alasdan.

published by

**Alan Fyfe on behalf of
the Edinburgh Academical Club**

2007

© Alasdair Macintyre, 2007

Published in Great Britain by

Alan Fyfe
Struan Cottage
Ratho, Scotland

on behalf of

The Edinburgh Academical Club
The Edinburgh Academy
42 Henderson Row
Edinburgh EH3 5BL

First edition, 2007

ISBN 0-9548764-2-3

Typeset in Minion Pro

Printed and bound by David Macdonald Ltd
25 Rodney Street, Edinburgh, EH7 4EL

Profits from the sale of this book are shared
between the Edinburgh Academy Foundation and
the Victoria Cross & George Cross Association.

CONTENTS

LIST OF ILLUSTRATIONS

FOREWORD

by Lieutenant-General Robert Baxter
Deputy Chief of Defence Staff (Health)

It is a privilege and singular honour to be asked to write a foreword on any publication about the Victoria Cross: it is particularly so to put pen to paper for a publication that honours the memory of Victoria Cross holders who were also fellow Academicals. The Victoria Cross holds a very special place in the heart of military men. Field Marshall Viscount Slim in *Courage and other Broadcasts* captured this when he said, 'I do not believe that there is any man who would not rather be called brave than have any other virtue attributed to him'.

The Victoria Cross is special for its rarity which stems from the conditions that have to be met for what is known as a Level One Award. Namely 'for most conspicuous bravery, or some daring or pre-eminent act of valour or self sacrifice, or extreme devotion to duty in the presence of the enemy'. In the period since 1950 there have only been 13 awards of the Victoria Cross, 4 of them to soldiers from Australia and New Zealand. Sadly, of the most recent 4 awards to British soldiers, 3 have been posthumous, including the latest.

When you read accounts of the actions leading to the award it is important to understand the guidance and criteria that recommending officers are invited to consider. There are over 10 factors ranging from the threat and outcome to considerations of rank and experience, more would be expected from the more senior and experienced. The citations themselves might appear understated but again the direction is absolutely clear; plain English is to be used to describe in straightforward terms the conditions and circumstances surrounding the individual's actions, and hyperboles and unnecessary superlatives are to be eschewed.

It has always seemed to me that simplicity is a key theme of this very special award: the dull bronze of the cross itself; its simple inscription, For Valour; and, the dull crimson ribbon. We have Queen Victoria herself and Prince Albert to thank for the simplicity of the name, the proposition was for the Military Order of Victoria. The award is of course open to all ranks.

As is probably well known the medal is cast from the bronze of captured cannons. In these days of the relentless pursuit of efficiency, I trust that this represents an excellent example of thriftiness! It may be an apocryphal story but in a recent 'housekeeping' exercise to clear out stores of materiel that had not moved for a very long time the lump of bronze was, not unexpectedly right at the top of slow moving items and, so the story goes, very nearly sold to a scrap merchant.

When one reads accounts of those who have earned the Victoria Cross the themes of modesty, of doing one's job, of selflessness, all come to the fore. This theme was well made in the Archbishop of Canterbury's address at the inauguration of the Victoria Cross and George Cross Memorial in 2003 when he said: 'Courage as a true virtue is the kind of courage that reflects the bravery of Christ, courage that does not deny the reality of fear but is energised by vision'. I suppose that it is not surprising that so many recipients have been members of the medical or chaplaincy services.

Putting people on a pedestal these days as an example invites the active attention of the debunker but those who have earned the Victoria Cross are in a rather special category. So I commend Alasdair Macintyre's short publication on a very particular group of brave Academicals.

Floreat Academia.

Robert Baxter (EA 1965-1971)
August 2007

In memory of my father
David Lowe Macintyre, VC, CB
(1895-1967)

PROLOGUE

The elderly, white-haired gentleman pauses for a moment in the yards of his old school, looking up at the impressive sandstone building which is the gymnasium. It had been built years ago as a memorial to all those Academicals who had perished during the Great War. It is first a practical building, a fully equipped gym catering for the physical training needs of the pupils, but it has also been used as an examination hall and as an art gallery at the end of year exhibition. In the basement is the design and technology department, though in days gone by, the dusty nooks held a woodworking shop, a pottery studio, a music room, an armoury, and much more. But the gentleman is not interested in those today – he knows them full well. His eyes are squinting up at the brass plaques flanking the entrance – plaques listing the names of his fellow Academicals who did not return from war service.

He notices that one of those names, Walter Brodie, has a couple of inscribed initials next to it — they are 'VC'. Walter received this highest military decoration for gallantry in the war before he was killed in a later action. Scanning the plaques, he sees that this is the only Victoria Cross mentioned and he realises that this is because the war memorial only lists those who died in the two world wars. There are others who won the VC in actions in the last century and there are others in the twentieth century who lived to tell the tale.

The gentleman runs a hand through his white hair and pulls his overcoat more closely around his shoulders. He gives a slight shiver – it may be the cold, or it may be his memories.

INTRODUCTION

The Victoria Cross

The notion of giving a bravery award to low-ranking soldiers and sailors first came under serious consideration in Britain in 1854. Until that time, the government and the military leaders had not felt the need to reward 'ordinary' men for their courage. Even the great military leaders such as the Duke of Wellington had believed that serving monarch and country was reward enough for any low-ranking soldier or sailor. After nearly forty years of peace, Britain was embroiled in a major war with Russia in the Crimea, and from the earliest days of the conflict stories began to circulate of the outstanding bravery of the British Army in the most appalling conditions. Their heroics were performed despite a lack of adequate clothing and other provisions to protect them from the harsh Russian winter, and hospitals tending to the wounded were dire. There was a general clamour that something needed to be done to recognise the efforts of rank-and-file British servicemen who were risking their lives thousands of miles from home.

Both Queen Victoria and Prince Albert were enthusiastic about addressing the problem, particularly as the enemy, Russia, already had awards for gallantry that ignored rank. Shortly after the start of the war, the Distinguished Conduct Medal (DCM) was instituted for NCOs and privates, and a campaign medal for the Crimean War was approved. It was the Duke of Newcastle, the Secretary of State for War, who seized the initiative in 1855, writing to Prince Albert: 'It does not seem right or politic to me that such deeds of heroism as the war has produced should go unrewarded by any distinctive outward mark of honour because they are done by privates or by officers below the rank of major...' The Duke broke the news of a radical new bravery award to the public when he told the House of Lords nine days later that the government had advised the Queen 'to institute a cross of merit which would be open to all ranks of the Army in future'.

The VC was founded by a Royal Warrant issued on 29th January

1856, which announced the creation of a single decoration available to the British Army and the Royal Navy. It was intended to reward 'individual instances of merit and valour' and which 'we are desirous should be highly prized and eagerly sought after'. The warrant laid down fifteen rules and ordinances that had to be inviolably observed and kept.

The first presentation of the award was made in Hyde Park, London, on 26th June 1857 when Queen Victoria decorated 62 officers and men for their actions in the Crimea, in front of a crowd of about a hundred thousand people.

Lord Ashcroft's Victoria Cross Collection

About twenty years ago, Michael Ashcroft bought his first Victoria Cross. Today the Michael Ashcroft Trust, which was established to care for and protect the VC collection, now owns 145 Victoria Crosses, just over a tenth of the 1356 that have been awarded to individuals since 1856. It is by far the largest collection in the world. The Trust has plans to open its collection to the public when a suitable location can be found.

Edinburgh Academicals

According to Bill Stirling's book, *175 Accies*, Edinburgh Academicals have been awarded a total of nine Victoria Crosses, a statistic that is confirmed in Magnus Magnusson's book *The Clacken and the Slate*. The medals of three of them (James Dundas, John Cook and Allan Ker) are held in the Ashcroft Collection. Of the remainder, four are held in military museums, as noted in the text, and the other two are not publicly held.

The actions for which the awards were made range in time from the Indian Mutiny (1857-1858) through to World War II (1939-1945). Three were won in the Indian Mutiny, one in the Bhutan War (1864-1865), one in the Afghan wars (1878-1880), one in the Second Boer War (1899-1902), two in World War I (1914-1918) and one in World War II.

In the first half of the nineteenth century, the East India Company maintained its own private army, and most officers of that army trained at two military colleges or seminaries.

The first of these, the Edinburgh Military and Naval Academy, opened in 1825 and was located in various premises, including

Waterloo Place, St. James Square and George Street. In time, however, premises became available through the Royal Riding Academy leasing part of its property in Lothian Road, opposite the entrance to King's Stables Road and Castle Terrace. The Edinburgh Military and Naval Academy moved there in 1830. Following the end of the Indian Mutiny, the abolition of the East India Company, and the transference of its civil and military branches to the Crown in 1858, the Academy fell into decline and eventually ceased to function. In 1869 the building was demolished to make way for the Caledonian Railway Station, and the site is now occupied by part of the Caledonian Hotel.

South of the border, the East India Company, in 1809, bought Addiscombe Place in Croydon, Surrey, and created there a military seminary. The original house was built in 1702 to Vanburgh's design. The Company maintained its own army and officers were trained there before setting off to India. After the East India Company ceased to exist, the seminary at Addiscombe Place closed. It was sold to developers in 1863 and they, regrettably, razed it to the ground with dynamite.

The Victoria Cross & George Cross Association

At the 1956 centenary of the creation of the Victoria Cross, 299 recipients of the medal were gathered together from all parts of the world, the focal point being the review of holders in Hyde Park by Her Majesty the Queen on 26th June. It was during these celebrations that the decision was made to form the Victoria Cross Association with its main aims and objective being the provision of a headquarters to provide communication with each other and thereby give help and guidance to one another when required. In order to cement the fellowship amongst the membership, regular reunions have been held every other year, and the resulting strength of friendship has been of comfort and help to all. George Cross holders became associate members in 1957, and in 1961 they were invited to become full members and the association renamed.

The association is a registered charity and has a benevolent fund, which provides financial assistance to members and the widows of past members when necessary. This fund also provides grants towards the restoration or replacement of headstones or other memorials of past recipients of the Victoria Cross and George Cross.

The writer was privileged to attend the service of dedication of the Victoria Cross and George Cross Memorial at Westminster Abbey on 14th May 2003 and the service of commemoration to mark the 150th anniversary of the institution of the Victoria Cross at Westminster Abbey on 26th June 2006.

Acknowledgements

I am grateful to have been given access to the many sources of information that exist on the holders, and am particularly indebted to the following: Doug Arman, Vic Tambling and Paul Oldfield of the Victoria Cross Database Users Group; Max Arthur for permission to quote liberally from his book, *Symbol of Courage – A Complete History of the Victoria Cross*; the Michael Ashcroft Trust for permission to quote from Michael Ashcroft's book *Victoria Cross Heroes*; Mrs Didy Grahame, MVO of the Victoria Cross & George Cross Association; *Firepower*, the Royal Artillery Museum, Woolwich; the 14th/20th King's Hussars Museum, Preston, Lancashire; the Local History Centre, East Lothian Council, Haddington; the Highland Council Reference Library, Inverness; Stuart Allan, Senior Curator of Military History, National Museums of Scotland in Edinburgh; and the great grand niece of John Cook, VC, Diana Cook, who has been helpful and enthusiastic about this project from the start.

Pictures of several of the Academicals have been reproduced by kind permission of *This England* magazine (publishers of the *Register of the Victoria Cross*). That of James Hills has been reproduced from the web site www.haileybury.herts.sch.uk/archives/roll/heic vc.htm, taken in turn from *The VC & DSO Book* on which the copyright has expired. That of Anthony Miers is taken from the book *The Freemen of Inverness*, by W. J. Mackay; attempts to find the copyright ownership of this book have proved futile. The map of the Western Front is redrawn with permission from an original in Max Arthur's book, *Symbol of Courage*.

I am also grateful to my editor, Alan Fyfe, without whom my work would still be an assortment of jumbled notes; Alan also helped me with research into place names and compiled the maps. And lastly, but by no means least, I would like to give heartfelt thanks to Lieutenant-General Robert Baxter for agreeing to write the foreword and to Clifford Koch (EA 1958-69) for volunteering to pen me a prologue.

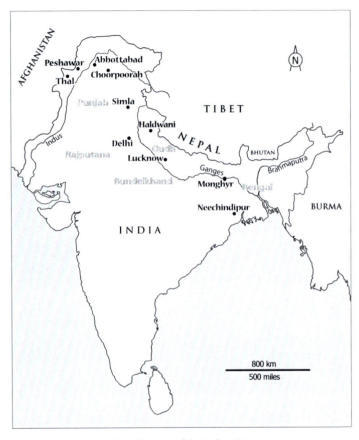

India at the time of the Indian Mutiny
with some of the places mentioned in the text

THE INDIAN MUTINY 1857-1858

Campaign Background

Although it was ultimately unsuccessful, the Indian or Sepoy Mutiny against colonial rule in India tested Britain's military resources to the limits. The ferocious and sustained uprisings across the north of India, which began in May 1857 and lasted until late 1858, afforded many situations in which British and native soldiers demonstrated extreme courage in the face of the enemy.

The Siege of Delhi

Control of Delhi was the key to putting down the rebellion, so all available troops were called in. The Delhi Field Force of four thousand British, Sikh and Pathan troops approached the city, and sent out to meet them was a force of thirty thousand mutineers with thirty guns. They met in a battle on 8th June 1857, but the Delhi Field Force was able to occupy the strategically important area of the ridge to the north-west of the city walls.

It was in June and July that Thomas Cadell and James Hills were in the actions for which they were awarded the Victoria Cross.

Uprisings in the North, September 1857 to February 1858

From September 1857 to February 1858 troops were called to put down uprisings throughout the north, including at Choorpoorah, which was where John Adam Tytler was in the action for which he was awarded the Victoria Cross.

1.

THOMAS CADELL, VC, CB
(EA 1845-1848)

born on 5th September 1835 in East Lothian

died on 6th April 1919 in Edinburgh

Citation

The award of the Victoria Cross to Thomas Cadell, for action at Flagstaff Picquet and at Metcalfe's House, during the Siege of Delhi, India, on 12 June 1857, was published on p. 2229 of *London Gazette* No. 22621, dated 29th April 1862.

The late 2nd European Bengal Fusiliers Lieutenant Thomas Cadell

Date of Acts of Bravery, 12th June 1857

For having, on the 12th June, 1857, at the Flagstaff Picquet at Delhi, when the whole of the Picquet of Her Majesty's 75th Regiment and 2nd European Bengal Fusiliers were driven in by a large body of the enemy, brought in from amongst the enemy a wounded Bugler of his own Regiment, under a most severe fire, who would otherwise have been cut up by the rebels. Also, the same day, when the Fusiliers were retiring, by order, on Metcalfe's House, on its being reported that there was a wounded man left behind, Lieutenant Cadell went back of his own accord towards the enemy, accompanied by three men, and brought a man in of the 75th Regiment, who was severely wounded, under a most heavy fire from the advancing enemy.

Thomas Cadell was decorated with the Victoria Cross by Brigadier-General James Travers at a grand parade at Saugor, India on 19th November 1862. The medal is not publicly held.

Thomas was born at Cockenzie House, Cockenzie, East Lothian on 5th September 1835, tenth child of twelve (six sons and six daughters) of Hew Francis Cadell, landed proprietor, and Jane Marian Buchan-Sydserff. Thomas attended the Academy from 1845-1848, in classes 1–3 and then the Grange School, Sunderland. He was at school in Holland before entering the Military Academy. He was a contemporary of James Hills (see p. 16) whilst at the Edinburgh Academy.

Service Career

Thomas was gazetted 2nd lieutenant in 1854 to the 2nd European Bengal Fusiliers (later the Royal Munster Fusiliers) and his first service was in Burma. He was stationed in India when the Indian Mutiny broke out and took part in the Siege of Delhi in 1857. He served throughout the Oudh Campaign between 1858 and 1859

Cockenzie House, East Lothian, home of the Cadell family. The building is now a Nursing Home

with the 4th Irregular Cavalry and commanded a flying column in Bundlekhund against the Bheels between 1859 and 1860. He was mentioned in despatches and received the thanks of the Governor-General in Council for his services.

He was promoted captain on 17th April 1866, major on 17th April 1874, lieutenant-colonel on 17th April 1880, and colonel on 17th April 1884. He was placed on the unemployed supernumerary list on 5th September 1892.

He afterwards entered the Political Department, and held various appointments in Central India. He was governor of the Andaman and Nicobar Islands from 1879 to 1892.

Marriage and Family

Thomas Cadell married Anna Catherine Dalmahoy, daughter of Patrick Dalmahoy and Anna Catherine Sawers, on 18th April 1867 in Edinburgh. Anna was the sister of Ensign Patrick Carfrae Dalmahoy of the 60th Native Infantry. He was also a pupil at the Edinburgh Academy (1850-1854) and saw extensive action throughout the Indian Mutiny, including with Thomas at the Siege of Delhi. Thomas and Anna had seven children, five sons and two daughters, all born in India. Anna predeceased her husband on 31st August 1876.

Post-Military Life

On his return home from the Andaman Islands, Colonel Cadell settled in Cockenzie and devoted himself to public affairs in East Lothian. True to his family traditions, he was guide, philosopher and friend to the fishing community of the district. The cause of education throughout the county owes much to his unflagging zeal, as the opening up of large endowments for educational purposes was largely due to him. The care of the poor was his care and he was in constant attendance at county meetings in his capacity as county councillor. He was an active and zealous member of the United Free Church in Cockenzie and, from 1907 to 1919, was on the Court of Directors of the Edinburgh Academy.

In 1906, he was made a Companion of the Order of the Bath for his services in India.

Death and funeral

Colonel Thomas Cadell, VC, CB died on 6th April 1919 at 25 Walker Street, Edinburgh and was survived by two sons and two daughters.

His funeral took place with full military honours from Cockenzie United Free Church, where a service was held, to the family burial vaults in Tranent churchyard. The service was conducted by Brigadier-General the Rev. Dr. Mackay and the Rev. J. Hastie, and there was a large attendance. The coffin was carried into the church by a number of representative fishermen from the village, and a simultaneous memorial service was held in St. Andrew's Church, Drumsheugh Gardens, Edinburgh. Amongst those in attendance at Cockenzie was Mr. R. H. Ferard, Rector of Edinburgh Academy. At the conclusion of the service in Cockenzie Church, the coffin was placed on a gun carriage driven by officers of the Royal Field Artillery. Three hundred men of the Argyll and Sutherland Highlanders were in attendance, with pipers and drummers, while along the route to Tranent there was a large turnout of spectators.

The coffin having been born to the grave-side by the fishermen, Brigadier-General the Rev. Dr. Mackay conducted the committal ceremony, which was followed by the firing of three volleys, the sounding of *The Last Post* and the playing of a dirge.

Memorials

Thomas is commemorated in three places, the most impressive being the beacon memorial at Port Seton harbour. *The Haddingtonshire Courier* of 18th February 1921 described its dedication:

> Much interest was manifested in Cockenzie and Port Seton on Saturday afternoon in the unveiling of a memorial to the late Colonel Thomas Cadell, VC, CB of Cockenzie whose kindly helpful influence and work are so affectionately remembered by all inhabitants. The memorial takes the appropriate form of a beacon light and is erected at the harbour entrance in proximity to the existing beacon which has done service for more than forty years and which will now be dismantled. The light is erected on an elegant pillar with a handsome base, and in front, it bears the following inscription:- 'Erected 1921 by the Cockenzie and Port Seton fishermen, and other friends, in memory of Colonel Thomas Cadell, VC, CB of Cockenzie; born 5th September 1835; died 5th April 1919'.

There is also a memorial plaque in his honour in Chalmers Memorial Church, Port Seton, and his name is on the VC Roll of Honour at the Union Jack Club, Sandell Street, Waterloo, London.

Thomas Cadell's beacon memorial at Port Seton harbour

Brothers of Thomas Cadell

Three of Thomas's five brothers were educated at the Edinburgh Academy and had significant careers and some notes on them are given here. Of the other two, William George Cadell, born in 1823, died in 1836, and Charles Cadell, born in 1827, died in infancy.

John Cadell was born on 16th November 1819 at Cockenzie House and was educated at the Edinburgh Academy from 1829 to 1834. He became the Belgian Vice-Consul at Leith and died on 3rd January 1853.

Francis Cadell was born on 8th February 1822 at Cockenzie House and was educated at the Edinburgh Academy from 1830 to 1834, continuing his education in Germany. He went to sea as a midshipman on an East Indiaman in 1836 and took part in the Siege of Canton and the capture of Amoy and Ningpo in the First China War (1840-1841). He won honours and took a share of prize money, and was promoted to lieutenant, but was discharged shortly after for insubordination. He then returned home and studied shipbuilding and engineering in the shipyards of the Tyne and Clyde, before setting off trading in one of his father's ships to Europe, North America and then South America, where he skipped ship and went exploring the Amazon River. He eventually travelled to Australia in 1848 where he turned his attention to the navigation of the Murray River. Sir Henry Young, the then governor of South Australia, offered a financial bonus for the first two steamers that should successfully navigate the Murray from the town of Goolwa to the junction of the Darling River.

Cadell returned to Australia in 1850 and started from Melbourne with a canvas boat carried on a packhorse. He launched his craft at Swan Hill Station, on the Upper Murray, and, with four gold-diggers as his companions, commenced a voyage of many hundreds of miles. His examination of the river convinced him that there would be little difficulty on navigating it with steamers, and his representations on this subject on his arrival in Adelaide led to the formation of the Murray Steam Navigating Company. The first steamship of the company's fleet was called *Lady Augusta*, after the wife of the governor. On her voyage up the Murray on 25th August 1853, she was commanded by Francis Cadell. The *Lady Augusta* reached Swan Hill on 17th September, a distance of 1,300 miles from her starting point, and returned thence with the first cargo of wool that had been floated on the Murray. At a banquet given by Sir Henry Young in Adelaide, a gold candelabrum of the value of 900 guineas, with a commemorative inscription was handed to Cadell. At the same time, three gold medals were struck by order of the legislature of South Australia, and one of them was given to Cadell.

He continued his explorations over a number of years, all the while opening up extended routes up into New South Wales, and his labours contributed to the development of the resources of the colony of Australia. However, he derived very little substantial reward from them. The sums granted in aid of his explorations were utterly inadequate to cover the expenses incurred, and in his eagerness to serve the public, his attention was distracted from commercial pursuits. The Murray Steam Navigation Company was dissolved and Cadell, having lost all his money, retired to the bush and began life as a settler on a small station near Mount Murchison, on the Darling River.

In November 1867, when exploring in South Australia, he discovered the mouth of the River Roper and a tract of fine pastoral country, but the concurrence of bad seasons and misfortunes induced him to undertake a trading voyage to the Spice Islands. He sailed in his schooner, *Gem*, fitted with auxiliary steam-power and was on passage from Amboyna to the Kei Islands, when he was murdered by his crew, who afterwards sank the vessel. This tragic event, which put an end to the career of one of the most enterprising and honourable men, took place in June 1879. Cadell Street in Goolwa, South Australia was named after him.

Robert Cadell was born on 13th February 1825 at Cockenzie House and was educated at the Edinburgh Academy from 1834 to 1840. He was in the Royal Artillery, and entered the Madras Artillery in 1842. He was colonel-commandant in 1885, and served in the Crimean War and the Indian Mutiny. He was inspector-general of ordnance in Madras from 1877 to 1881 and later was a justice of the peace and a county councillor for East Lothian.

On 26th November 1889, he married Elizabeth Douglas Cunningham, daughter of Rev. William Bruce Cunningham, Minister of the Free Church in Cockenzie and Cecilia Margaret Douglas. He was knighted in 1894 and, as General Sir Robert Cadell, died on 30th June 1897 at Cockenzie House. His wife died on 17th June 1910 at 19 Hatton Place, Edinburgh.

The Roll of Honour in the Union Jack Club,
Sandell Street, Waterloo, London

2.

JAMES HILLS, VC, GCB
(later HILLS-JOHNES)
(EA 1843-1847)

born on 20th August 1833 in Bengal, India

died on 3rd January 1919 in Carmarthenshire

Citation

The award of the Victoria Cross, for action at the Ridge, Delhi, during the Siege of Delhi, India, on 9th July 1857, was published on p. 2050 of *London Gazette* No. 22131, dated 24th April 1858.

> *Bengal Artillery... Lieutenant-Colonel Henry Tombs, CB and Lieutenant James Hills*
>
> *Date of Acts of Bravery, 9th July 1857*
>
> For very gallant conduct on the part of Lieutenant Hills before Delhi, in defending the position assigned to him in case of alarm, and for noble behaviour on the part of Lieutenant-Colonel Tombs in twice coming to his subaltern's rescue, and on each occasion killing his man. [1]

James was decorated with the Victoria Cross by Sir Colin Campbell, Commander-in-Chief India in 1858. His medal is held at *Firepower*, the Royal Artillery Museum, Woolwich.

James Hills was born at Neechindipur, Bengal, India on 20th August 1833, tenth child of eleven (seven sons and four daughters) of James Hills and Charlotte Mary Savi. James attended the Academy from 1843-1847 in classes 2–5. He would have been a contemporary of Thomas Cadell (see p. 8). He attended the Royal Military College, Edinburgh, and Addiscombe Military Seminary, Croydon, from 1851-1853.

Service Career

James was commissioned 2nd lieutenant in the Bengal Artillery on 11th June 1853. He served in the Indian Mutiny and was promoted

---

[1] Note regarding James Hills's action: during the Siege of Delhi, whilst on picket duty with two guns on a hill near the camp, his force was suddenly attacked by rebel cavalry. Without hesitation, he rode straight at the enemy, single-handed, in order to cause a commotion and give the guns time to load. He cut down two rebels before being thrown from his horse by two sowars charging together. Now on foot, he managed to fight off two more assailants and was about to be killed by a third when Major Tombs came to his assistance.

lieutenant on 8th September 1857. He took part in action at the siege and capture of Lucknow in March 1858, Fort Rooya, the Battle of Bareilly and the relief of Shahjehanpur in 1858.

He was appointed aide-de-camp to Lord Canning, governor general and viceroy of India from September 1859 to 1862, was promoted captain on 24th November 1860 and given the brevet of major on 19th January 1864. He was appointed brigade major of the Royal Artillery, Northern Division, Bengal from 1864 to 1869.

James sailed from Calcutta aboard the P & O steamer *Golconda* on 9th January 1868 to take part in the Abyssinian Expedition of 1867-1868 as officer commanding an 8-inch mortar battery and was present at the capture of Magdala. He was given the brevet of lieutenant-colonel on 15th August 1868, given the brevet of colonel on 14th February 1876 and was appointed assistant-adjutant-general of the Lahore Division from 1876 to 1879. He was promoted major-general on 10th July 1879 and lieutenant-general on 26th January 1886. He retired from the Army in 1888.

Marriage and Family

James Hills married Elizabeth Johnes on 16th September 1882 at Westminster Abbey, London. Elizabeth had been christened on 9th July 1834 at Cynwyl Gaeo, Carmarthen, Wales. James assumed by royal licence the additional name and arms of Johnes, by reason of his marriage with Elizabeth who was co-heiress of the late John Johnes, of Dolaucothy, Carmarthenshire.

Post-Military Life

James was a justice of the peace and deputy lieutenant for Carmarthenshire and held the post of honorary colonel of various Welsh regiments. He was made a Freeman of the County and Burgh of Carmarthenshire in 1910 and, in 1917, the University of Wales conferred on him the honorary degree of LLD. James Hills-Johnes died at Dolaucothy, Carmarthenshire on 3rd January 1919. His widow, Elizabeth, died on 9th April 1927.

Other citations

He was awarded the Insignia of a Companion of the Order of the Bath (*London Gazette* 10th September 1872), KCB (*London Gazette* 22nd February 1881) and GCB (*London Gazette* 2nd June 1893).

Memorials

James is commemorated in three places. Firstly, in Caio Church, Carmarthenshire, there is a plaque on the wall inside the church. There is also a memorial on the wall near his grave and his name is engraved on the Church Lych gate.

He also has a memorial in St. George's Garrison Church, Woolwich, London and his name is on the VC Roll of Honour at the Union Jack Club, Sandell Street, Waterloo, London.

Brothers of James Hills

Four of James's brothers were also educated at the Edinburgh Academy and some notes on their careers are given here. The other two brothers, Elliot and Charles, had died in infancy.

Archibald Hills was born on 3rd March 1832 and christened on 10th April 1832 at Chandernagore, West Bengal, India. He was educated at the Edinburgh Academy from 1843 to 1847. In 1860, he married Emma Louisa Gale White in Bengal, India and they had four children, all born between 1862 and 1870 in India.

John Hills was born on 19th August 1834 in Bombay, Maharashtra, India, and was educated at the Edinburgh Academy from 1844 to 1847 and afterwards at Edinburgh University. He then entered Addiscombe College on 6th August 1852 and was gazetted 2nd lieutenant in the Bombay Engineers on 8th June 1854.

He had basic instruction at Brompton Barracks, Chatham, Kent and arrived at Bombay in August 1856, where he was posted to the Bombay Sappers and Miners. He was passed in Hindustani and appointed assistant field engineer with the 2nd division of the Persian Expeditionary Force under Major General Sir James Outram on 14th January 1857. He was present at the capture of Mohumra, promoted lieutenant on 5th November 1857 and was also elected a Fellow of the Royal Society of Edinburgh on 21st March 1859.

John was appointed garrison engineer at Fort William, Calcutta and in January 1862 became assistant to the chief engineer in Oudh in the Public Works Department at Lucknow. He was promoted to captain on 1st September 1863 and was appointed executive engineer in Rajputana in 1865. He joined the Abyssinian Expedition under Major-General Sir Robert Napier in 1867 where he was first employed as field engineer at Kumeyli camp to which the railway was made from Kumeyli to Senafeh. He was mentioned in despatches.

John returned to Lucknow where he was assumed command of the Bombay Sappers and Miners at Kirkee from 1871 to 1883. He was promoted major on 5th July 1872, lieutenant-colonel on 1st October 1877 and given the brevet of colonel on 1st October 1881.

He assumed command of a division of the Kandahar Field Force as well as of the South Afghanistan Field Force during the Afghan War of 1879-1880. He took part in the defence of Kandahar and was mentioned in despatches for his services and created CB on 22nd February 1881. He assumed command of the expeditionary force to Burma in 1886-1887 and retired on 31st December 1887 with the honorary rank of major-general. He was created KCB in May 1900. He was an all-round sportsman, excelling at cricket, swimming, swordsmanship and shooting. He died unmarried at 50 Weymouth Street, London on 18th June 1902 and was buried in the family vault at Kensal Green.

George Scott Hills was born on 16th September 1835 at Neechindipur, Bengal, India and was educated at the Edinburgh Academy from 1844 to 1847. He also joined the Army and became a colonel in the Royal Artillery. He died on 11th May 1892.

Robert Savi Hills was born on 8th May 1837 at Neechindipur, Bengal, India and was educated at the Edinburgh Academy from 1850 to 1853. Robert was described in his marriage certificate as a merchant. He married Agnes Leonore Hay on 8th January 1896 at Dyce, Aberdeenshire and they had four daughters and three sons. Subsequently, they are known to have lived at Rattray House, Crimond, at Nethermuir House, New Deer, Aberdeenshire, at Kirktophill, Marykirk, Kincardineshire, and finally at Manar House, Inverurie, Aberdeenshire, where he died on 5th January 1909. He was here described as a retired planter. His wife, Agnes, died on 22nd January 1940 in Montrose, Angus.

Related holders of the Victoria Cross

James's sister Charlotte Isabella Hills was born at Neechindipur, Bengal, India and in 1863 she married Colonel William George Cubitt in Calcutta. William, then a lieutenant in the 13th Bengal Native Infantry was in action on 30th June 1857 when he had been sent from the Lucknow Residency as part of a force to fight the advancing rebels. He showed great courage in this ill-fated contest and when the retreat from Lucknow began, he saved the lives of three men as the rebels were surging round him, for which he was awarded the Victoria Cross. He had also been awarded the DSO. He died in 1903 at Camberley, Surrey.

James's sister, Emilia Savi Hills, was christened at Kishnagur, Bengal, India on 10th January 1849 and in 1873 she married Sir Griffith Evans, KCIE, JP, DL. Of their family, one son, Lewis Pugh Evans, while an acting lieutenant-colonel with the Black Watch, commanding 1st Battalion Lincolnshire Regiment, was in action on 4th October 1917 near Zonnebeke, Belgium. Whilst leading his battalion through terrific enemy barrage, he rushed single-handed a machine-gun emplacement, which was causing casualties and caused its garrison to surrender by firing his revolver through the loophole. He was twice badly wounded but refused treatment until a further two objectives had been captured. He then collapsed from loss of blood. For this action, he was awarded the Victoria Cross. He later achieved the rank of brigadier-general and was also awarded CB, CMG, DSO and Bar. He died in 1962 at Paddington, London.

3.

JOHN ADAM TYTLER, VC, CB
(EA 1838-1840)

born on 29th October 1825 in Bengal, India

died on 14th February 1880 at Thal on the North-West Frontier

Citation

The award of the Victoria Cross, for action at Choorpoorah, India, on 10th February 1858, was published on p. 3903 of *London Gazette* No. 22176, dated 24th August 1858.

66th (Ghoorkha) Bengal Native Infantry Lieutenant John Adam Tytler
Date of Act of Bravery 10th February 1858

On the attacking parties approaching the enemy's position under a heavy fire of round shot, grape and musketry, on the occasion of the action at Choorpoorah, on 10th February last, Lieutenant Tytler dashed on horseback ahead of all, and alone, up to the enemy's guns, where he remained engaged hand to hand, until they were carried by us; and where he was shot through the left arm, had a spear wound on his chest, and a ball through the right sleeve of his coat. (letter from Captain C. C. G. Ross, Commanding 66th (Ghoorkha) Regiment, to Captain Brownlow, Major of Brigade, Kemoan Field Force).

He was decorated with the Victoria Cross in India in 1858. His medal is held at the Gurkha Museum at Winchester, Hampshire.

John Adam Tytler was born at Monghyr, Bengal, India on 29th October 1825, son of John Tytler, surgeon of the Honourable East India Company Service and Anne Gillies. He was educated at Mr De Joux's Day School, St.Helier, Jersey and at the Edinburgh Academy from 1838-1840 in classes 3–4.

Service Career

Commissioned into the Honourable East India Company in December 1843, he sailed for India, where he started service as a cadet in the Bengal Native Army on 27th November 1844. He was appointed ensign on 10th December 1844, posted to the 66th Goorkha Regiment on 14th March 1845, and was promoted lieutenant on 19th July 1848.

John saw active service on the Peshawar front under Sir Colin Campbell in 1851, and was appointed adjutant in October 1853. He served in the Indian Mutiny in 1857-1859, including the defence of the Kumoan Hills, and took part in action at Haldwani, Rohilkund and in the Oudh Campaign.

He saw action at Choorpoorah, in which he was wounded and for which he was awarded his Victoria Cross. He was evacuated to hospital but recovered sufficiently to take part in the closing scenes of the suppression of the Mutiny.

He was promoted captain on 2nd April 1859 and served in the Umbeyla Expedition of 1863, where he assumed command of his regiment, the 4th Gurkhas, an appointment he retained until his death in 1880. He was present at action in the Umbeyla Pass, including the assault and capture of Conical Hill and the villages of Lalloo and Umbeyla. For his services he was mentioned in despatches.

He was promoted major on 10th December 1864 and appointed commandant of the 4th Gurkha Rifles on 4th December 1865. He led his regiment in the Hazara Expedition, and again he was mentioned in despatches.

Promoted lieutenant-colonel on 10th December 1870, he took part in the Lushai Expedition between 1871 and 1872 and for his services in this campaign he was created CB. He was given brevet of colonel in the Bengal Staff Corps on 10th December 1875.

He was promoted brigadier-general and appointed brigade commander of the Kurak Force in the North-West Frontier under Brigadier-General John Watson, VC. Watson accompanied Tytler as the Political Officer.

He took part in the Afghan War and was present at the fall of Ali Musjid (see map on p. 34), at which he commanded one of the flanking brigades and was given responsibility for maintaining communications between Sir Samuel Browne's force and Peshawar. During this time he twice led his brigade into the Afridi in order to control certain sections of the turbulent clans who were harassing convoys in the neighbourhood of the Khyber Pass. He went on to defeat the Shinwaris in a sharp engagement.

He assumed command of the troops between Landi Kotal and the old frontier, following the Treaty of Gandamak, but ill-health forced him to resign from his brigade before the start of September 1879.

On learning of the massacre at the embassy at Kabul, Tytler, though not yet fully recovered, assumed command of the troops against the hostile Zaimukht as part of the Kohat Field Force. He was then considered the greatest master of mountain warfare in the Indian Army. Tytler conducted operations with consummate skill, carrying out frontal attack while personally leading a flanking assault which swept the Zaimukht from their rocky fastnesses, which were previously deemed impregnable. Tytler was never physically strong and the exposure and hardship of two winter campaigns took their toll on his system, already exacerbated by numerous war wounds. He contracted pneumonia and died at Thal, Kurram Valley, North-West Frontier on 14th February 1880. He was buried at Kohat Cemetery, India.

He was also remembered for the significant part he played in the conversion of raw Gurkha levies into one of the finest regiments in the Indian Army.

*Map of Bhutan showing the capital, Thimphu,
and Dewangiri on the border with India*

THE BHUTAN WAR (or DUAR WAR) 1864-65

Campaign Background

The Indian state of Bhutan lies just to the east of Nepal, and in 1864, following a civil war in the region, Britain, protecting her interests in her Indian Empire, sent a peace mission to restore order.

The leader of the victorious Punakha people had broken with the central administration and set up a rival government. The legitimate governor was deposed, so the British mission mediated, dealing alternately with the supporters of the deposed and the new government. The latter, however, rejected all British attempts to broker peace, so in November 1864, Britain declared war on the new Bhutan regime. It was an ill-matched contest, as Bhutan had no regular army.

On 30th April 1865, a sharp engagement at Dewangiri in the south-east of Bhutan drove the Bhutanese out of their positions, but the resistance of a stubborn pocket of about two hundred men prompted a courageous assault on their block-house by men of the Royal (later Bengal) Engineers. Lieutenant James Dundas was awarded his VC for his actions in this engagement.

4.

JAMES DUNDAS, VC
(EA 1852-1855)

born on 12th September 1842 in Edinburgh

died on 23rd December 1879 in Kabul, Afghanistan

Citation

The award of the Victoria Cross, for action at Dewangiri, Bhootan, Afghanistan on 30th April 1865, was published on p. 7107 of *London Gazette* No. 23338, dated 31st December 1867.

Royal (late Bengal) Engineers Major William Spottiswoode Trevor Lieutenant James Dundas for their gallant conduct at the attack on the block-house at Dewan-Giri, in Bhootan, on the 30th April 1865.

Major-General Tombs, CB, VC, the officer in command at the time, reports that a party of the enemy, from 180 to 200 in number, had barricaded themselves in the block-house in question, which they continued to defend after the rest of the position had been carried, and the main body was in retreat. The block-house, which was loop-holed, was the key of the enemy's position. Seeing no officer of the storming party near him, and being anxious that the place should be taken immediately, as any protracted resistance might have caused the main body of Bhooteas to rally, the British force having been fighting in a broiling sun on very steep and difficult ground for upwards of three hours, the general in command ordered these two Officers to show the way into the block-house. They had to climb up a wall which was 14 feet high, and then to enter the house, occupied by some 200 desperate men, head foremost through an opening not more than two feet wide between the top of the wall and the roof of the block-house.

Major-General Tombs states that on speaking to the Sikh soldiers around him, and telling them in Hindoostani to swarm up the wall, none of them responded to the call, until these two officers had shown them the way, when they followed with the greatest alacrity. Both of them were wounded.

He was decorated with the Victoria Cross by Major-General J. Fordyce, commanding the Presidency Division of the Bengal Army at Fort William, the Maidan, Calcutta, India on 23rd March 1868. James Dundas's medal is held as part of the Ashcroft Collection.

James Dundas was born on 12th September 1842 at 28 Abercrombie Place, Edinburgh, the second, and twin with brother Colin, of nine children (five sons and four daughters) of George Dundas, advocate, and Elizabeth MacKenzie. In the 1851 census, James (aged 8) is living at 9 Charlotte Square, Edinburgh with his parents and six other siblings. There are seven others living there ranging from a governess to an under nurse. This would be the year before he went to the Academy. James attended the Academy from 1852-1855 in classes 1-3, being in the same class for these three years as John Cook (see p. 36). He later attended Trinity College, Glenalmond and Addiscombe College, Croydon in 1859-1860.

Service Career

James was commissioned into the Bengal Royal Engineers as a lieutenant on 8th June 1860. He carried out his basic training at Brompton Barracks, Chatham, Kent, sailed for India in March 1862 and was posted to the headquarters of the Sappers and Miners at Rurki. He was then posted to the Public Works Department in Bengal, where he became an executive engineer.

James took part in the action at Dewangiri, Bhutan, his gallantry here resulting in he and Major William Spottiswoode Trevor being awarded the Victoria Cross. Trevor and Dundas were immediately recommended for the Victoria Cross by Major Tombs, VC, but the recommendation was not supported by the commander-in-chief, Sir William Mansfield, on the grounds that he wanted to discourage any precedent for unorthodox intervention in infantry battles by those whose business lay elsewhere — Trevor and Dundas were engineer officers. Trevor later wrote that 'in his [Mansfield's] opinion, Dundas as engineer officer had acted officiously and altogether out of order in entering at all into the struggle… In fact he considered we had been guilty of an irregularity, which, if repeated might prove seriously detrimental to the discipline of the Army and which he was determined not to encourage…' Eventually, however, the Governor-General's Council considered that Tombs was the best judge of the affair and forwarded the case to the commander-in-chief at the Horse Guards, albeit with Sir William's continuing disapproval. The commander-in-chief put it forward to HM the Queen and success finally came with publication of the awards in the *London Gazette* of 31st December 1867, nearly three years after the event.

He rejoined the Public Works Department after the Bhutan War and in 1871 he was appointed as a personal assistant to General Sir Alexander Taylor in the Public Works Department.

In 1878, he was severely burnt about the hands while rescuing an Indian trapped in a burning house in Simla (see map on p. 6). A house in the bazaar was on fire and the roof had partly fallen in and buried a native, to such an extent that he could not get out. Captain Dundas, who was passing, made an attempt to rescue the man, but was driven out of the place by the falling rubbish and by the smoke. He called for a volunteer from the crowd and an officer of the Royal Artillery responded, and between them they were successful.

He was specially selected to the secretariat of the government of India in the Public Works Department in 1879, but chose instead to join General Roberts's force in the Second Afghan War. During the time Roberts was securing his position at Sherpur outside Kabul, Dundas and Lieutenant Charles Nugent were both ordered to join General Macpherson's Force to aid the destruction of the line of forts held by the enemy on the south side of the British position at Sherpur. Both Dundas and Nugent were killed on 23rd December by a premature explosion whilst using an improvised fuse as there had been a shortage of serviceable manufactured ones. He was buried at Seah Sang Cemetery, near Sherpur, Afghanistan.

Memorials

James is commemorated in five places. There is a memorial to him in St. Mary's Cathedral, Edinburgh inscribed:

> To the memory of James Dundas, VC Royal Engineers of Ochtertyre, Perthshire who fell on December 23 1879 in Afghanistan in his Country's service. This tablet is dedicated by his brother Officers as a mark of their regard and admiration.

He is also commemorated by a plaque at Glenalmond School, Perthshire, in a stained glass window in Rochester Cathedral, Kent and his name is on the VC Roll of Honour and diary at the Union Jack Club, Sandell Street, Waterloo, London. Lastly, a bridge on a road between Kabul and Bagram was dedicated to his memory as this report from *UK Defence Today*, of 21st March 2002 tells:

Sappers dedicate new Afghan bridge to Victoria Cross hero

Royal Engineers serving with the International Security Assistance Force in Afghanistan have rebuilt a bridge on a key road between Kabul and Bagram, and dedicated it to the memory of a Royal Engineer VC holder killed in action nearby in 1879.

The road across the Shermali Plain links Bagram airfield, centre of much military and humanitarian assistance efforts with Kabul. However, an important bridge over a river five kilometres south of Bagram had been repeatedly damaged in the many conflicts and the crossing heavily mined. A nearby ford has been in use, but vehicles using it risk being swept away, especially as spring brings on the thaw, and mines are known to have been washed into the river bed, adding a further menace.

The Royal Engineers therefore set about providing a permanent new bridge. Experts from 524 Specialist Troop Royal Engineers drew up a design using locally available materials, and their plans were then put into effect by some thirty Sappers, mainly drawn from 51 Air Assault Squadron, Royal Engineers. The new bridge was completed in just thirteen days… The work completed, the crossing has been named 'the Dundas Bridge' in honour of a Royal Engineer Officer, Captain James Dundas, who fell in action near Kabul on 23 December 1879. James Dundas had won the Victoria Cross during the Bhutan Expedition in 1865, leading the attack on an enemy block-house.

Tributes

His death deeply affected the small team of Sapper officers at Sherpur. Dundas had earned a reputation for hard work. A junior officer, Lieutenant John Burn-Murdoch, called him "… a most anxious fellow… frightfully hard working… he does not give us subs enough to do of the work… always getting up at the most unearthly hours though not a coolie shows his face until some hours later."

Colonel Stansfeld wrote to his family, "He was naturally shy and reserved with strangers, but there was a peculiar charm about his manner and conversation that soon attracted men to him. His utter absence of self, his modesty, his consideration for others and his honest upright sterling character, endeared him to all of us who had the privilege of calling him a friend."

Sir Alexander Taylor, for whom Dundas had worked for some years, wrote of him, "In him the Corps has lost one of its 'very best'. A man of high abilities, well cultivated - a modest, high-minded English [sic] gentleman, brave, gentle and courteous, I do not know that he ever gave offence to anyone, far less do I believe that he ever had an enemy. To me he was an invaluable professional assistant, and I owe much to his varied and accurate engineering knowledge, to his trustworthy character and universal popularity."

Brothers of James Dundas

James's four brothers all attended the Edinburgh Academy.

Colin MacKenzie Dundas was born on 12th September 1842 (twin with brother James) at 28 Abercromby Place, Edinburgh, and attended the Edinburgh Academy from 1852 to 1855, in the same class as John Cook (see p. 36). He entered the Royal Navy and attained the rank of commander. He was also a justice of the peace. He married Agnes Wauchope at St. Paul's Chapel, York Place, Edinburgh on 4th January 1882 and they had nine children. Agnes died on 19th March 1901 and Colin died on 15th June 1911 at Craigarnhall, Dunblane and Lecropt Parish, Perthshire.

George Ralph Dundas was born on 26th July 1844 at 28 Abercromby Place, Edinburgh and was educated at the Edinburgh Academy from 1854 to 1858. George died, unmarried, in 1868.

William John Dundas was born on 16th March 1849 at 28 Abercromby Place, Edinburgh and attended the Edinburgh Academy from 1859 to 1865. He qualified LLD (Edin) and was Crown Agent for Scotland from 1895 to 1905 and from 1916 to 1919. He died, unmarried, on 9th July 1921 at 11 Drumsheugh Gardens, Edinburgh.

David Dundas was born on 8th June 1854 at 9 Charlotte Square, Edinburgh and was educated at the Edinburgh Academy from 1864 to 1871. He was at Balliol College, Oxford from 1872 to 1876 and graduated BA. After attending Edinburgh University from 1876 to 1878, he was called to the Scottish Bar in 1878. He was an advocate depute from 1890 to 1892 and interim sheriff of Argyll from 1896 to 1898. He was made a QC in 1897 and became Solicitor General for Scotland from 1903 to 1905. He was a senator of the College of Justice in Scotland 1905, deputy lieutenant for the county of the City of Edinburgh. He was awarded an LLD from Edinburgh University in 1909 and became a member of the University Court of Edinburgh University as assessor to Rt. Hon. A. J. Balfour, MP, Chancellor of the University.

He married Helen Wauchope, daughter of David Baird Wauchope, Wine Merchant, and Helen Ann Mure on 22nd July 1885 at St. Mary's Cathedral, Edinburgh. He died on 14th February 1922 at 11 Drumsheugh Gardens, Edinburgh.

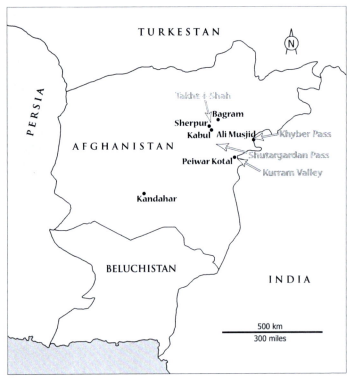

Afghanistan at the time of the Afghan Wars
with some of the places mentioned in the text

Note: borders tended to fluctuate - these are based on a map of 1889

THE SECOND & THIRD AFGHAN WARS 1878-80

Campaign Background

Britain had been keeping a watchful eye on this important buffer area to the north-west of British-ruled India as part of a policy of 'masterly inactivity'. In 1866 the Emir, Sher Ali, came to power. He was well disposed towards Britain and feared Russian encroachment in the region as much as Britain but, although prepared to support the Emir with arms and funds, Britain would promise no further help. In 1872, Britain and Russia had signed an agreement that the latter would respect Afghanistan's northern borders – there would be no need, the British Government thought, to give any promises of support to Afghanistan.

However, alarm bells sounded in the British corridors of power when, in 1876, Sher Ali reluctantly allowed a Russian mission to Kabul, and then, significantly, refused to admit Lord Lytton, sent out as viceroy, into the country. This Russian encroachment into central Asia was too close to British-ruled India to go unopposed. Lytton decided that Sher Ali must be removed – and when his ultimatum demanding that a British envoy be admitted to Kabul was ignored, three columns of British troops moved into Afghanistan in November 1878.

One of these columns, including the 5th Gurkha Rifles, under Major Frederick Roberts, set out along the Kurram Valley towards Kabul, but was met on 2nd December at Peiwar Kotal by an Afghan force of about eighteen thousand men and eleven guns. After a careful reconnaissance, Roberts made a dummy attack, under cover of darkness, leading his troops in a flanking movement to dislodge the Afghans, inflicting heavy injuries and capturing their guns.

5.

JOHN COOK, VC
(EA 1852-1856)

born on 28th August 1843 in Edinburgh

died on 19th December 1879 at Sherpur, Afghanistan

Citation

The award of the Victoria Cross, for action at Peiwar Kotal, Afghanistan, on 2nd December 1878, was published on p. 2241 of *London Gazette* No. 24697, dated 18th March 1879.

Bengal Staff Corps... Captain John Cook...

For a signal act of valour at the action of the Peiwar Kotal on the 2nd December 1878, in having, during a very heavy fire, charged out of the entrenchments with such impetuosity that the enemy broke and fled, when, perceiving, at the close of the melee, the danger of Major Galbraith, Assistant Adjutant-general, Kurum Column Field Force, who was in personal conflict with an Afghan soldier, Captain Cook distracted his attention to himself and aiming a sword cut which the Douranee avoided, sprang upon him, and, grasping his throat, grappled with him. They both fell to the ground. The Douranee, a most powerful man, still endeavouring to use his rifle, seized Captain Cook's arm in his teeth, until the struggle was ended by the man being shot in the head.

John Cook was decorated with the Victoria Cross by Major-General Frederick Roberts, VC at Ali Khel, Kurram on 24th May 1879 at a parade to mark the Queen's birthday, and in the presence of 6450 officers and men. John Cook's medal is held in the Ashcroft Collection.

John Cook was born on 28th August 1843 at 3 Darnaway Street, Edinburgh, second child of eight (six sons and two daughters) of Alexander Shank Cook, advocate, and Jane Stirling. In the 1851 census, John (age 7) is living at 31 North Castle Street, Edinburgh with his mother, aunt and four other siblings. There are three others living there – a governess, a cook and a house maid.

John Cook attended the Academy from 1852 to 1856 in classes 1–4, being in the same class for three years as James Dundas (see p. 28) and his twin brother, Colin (see p. 33). Thereafter, John attended the Scottish Naval and Military Academy, and Addiscombe College near Croydon.

Service Career

John Cook joined the Indian Army as an ensign from Addiscombe College in 1860 and almost immediately went to India. He was posted to Lucknow, Oudh, with the 4th Bengal Europeans in 1861 and transferred to the 107th Regiment in 1862. He was promoted lieutenant on 1st January 1862 in the Bengal Staff Corps and was posted to the 3rd Sikhs. He quickly distinguished himself in the battlefield, being mentioned in despatches for his service in the Umbeyla Campaign, as well as being thanked by his colonel for leading a courageous and effective bayonet charge. He was promoted to captain in 1872 and for the next six years served largely in India, transferring to the 5th Gurkhas in 1873.

He was involved in the reconnaissance of Peiwar Kotal, the first pass leading into Afghanistan on the Kurram side, then served under Major-General Frederick Roberts, VC, in a force which made a long night march in order to attack the enemy's left flank at dawn. However, the operation on 2nd December 1878 was sabotaged when two Afghans serving in the British force let off their rifles to warn their countrymen. The 5th Gurkhas had the lead position and, on reaching the enemy, Cook (in the words of his brother Lieutenant-Colonel Walter Cook), "charged out of the breastworks with such impetuosity that the enemy broke and fled". It was for his part in the following action (as described in the citation) that John Cook was awarded the Victoria Cross.

In skirmishes with the Afghans in December 1879, during which the Cook brothers led a bayonet charge, both men were wounded: John was brought to his knees by a heavy blow to the head, while Walter was shot in the chest. John recovered sufficiently to fight the next day but was again wounded, this time when a bullet passed through the bone in his left leg just below the knee. He had to spend the night in the open and, in the words of his brother, "the effect of this delay and exposure was to prove fatal". Initially, John thought he would lose his leg. However, his doctors procrastinated over the amputation and his condition deteriorated over the next few days. He died in hospital in Sherpur on 19th December 1879.

His death was announced in *Divisional Order* No. 2148 dated 21st December 1879, as follows:

It is with great regret that the lieutenant-colonel announces to the Kabul Force the death, from a wound received in action on the 12th December, of Major Cook, VC, 5th Gurkhas.

While yet a young officer, Major Cook served in Ambella in 1863, where he distinguished himself, and in the Black Mountain Campaign in 1868. Joining the Kurram Field Force at its formation, Major Cook was present at the capture of Peiwar Kotal, his conduct on that occasion earning him the admiration of the whole force and the Victoria Cross. Whilst in the action in the Monghyr Pass he again brought himself prominently to notice by his cool and gallant bearing. In the capture of the Takht-i-Shah peak on the 12th December he ended a noble career in a manner worthy of even his great name for bravery.

By Major Cook's death her Majesty has lost the services of an officer who would, had he been spared, have risen to the highest honours of his profession, and Sir Frederick Roberts feels sure the whole Kabul Field Force will share in the pain his loss has occasioned him.

John Cook was buried at Sherpur cantonment cemetery in the Church of England section on 21st December 1879. Those present at his funeral included General Sir Frederick Roberts, VC, Major George White, VC and Lieutenant William Dick-Cunyngham, VC.

In June 2004, Father Mark O'Keeffe CF (RC) serving with the HQ (UK) division in Afghanistan, visited the British cemetery at Kabul. By the standard of cemeteries in the sub-continent, the Kabul cemetery is in reasonable condition, considering that it contains British military gravestones dating back to the 1839-1842 occupation. The headstone of Major John Cook, VC, 5th Gurkha Rifles is still in very good condition.

Memorials

John Cook is commemorated by plaques in no less than four churches. The nearest to home is in St. Salvator's Chapel, St. Andrews, Fife. There are also plaques in St. Luke's Church, Chelsea, and in St. Paul's Cathedral, London. Finally, there is a plaque in St. Luke's Church, Abbottabad, Pakistan.

Walter and Elizabeth Cook, brother and sister, arranged for the erection of a family memorial in Warriston Cemetery, Edinburgh, in 1926. He is commemorated here and his name is on the VC Roll of Honour at the Union Jack Club, Sandell Street, Waterloo, London.

Brothers of John Cook

Four of John's brothers, all educated at the Edinburgh Academy, also had significant military careers. The other, Thomas, had died in infancy.

George Cook was born on 13th July 1842 at 3 Darnaway Street, Edinburgh, and attended the Edinburgh Academy from 1852 to 1858. He served as a lieutenant in the 77th Regiment and died unmarried from cholera at Peshawar, India on 18th June 1867. He maintained a series of diaries during his lifetime, ending just a few days before his death with the news that there was cholera in the camp.

Alexander Cook was born on 5th November 1847, also at 3 Darnaway Street, Edinburgh, and attended the Edinburgh Academy from 1858 to 1860. He entered the Royal Navy and served as lieutenant aboard *HMS Rapid* from 6th July 1871 to 31st January 1875, *HMS Sirius* from September 1875 to February 1880, *HMS Iris* from September 1880 to November 1882, when he was promoted commander.

From February 1884 to July 1885, he served as commander in Admiral Hewitt's flagship *Euryalus* in the Red Sea in connection with the Sudan insurrection, for which he received the Egyptian Medal and Khedive's Bronze Star. In 1886 he was appointed commander of *HMS Flagship Duke of Wellington* at Portsmouth, Hampshire.

Alexander Cook RN died suddenly at Southsea, Hampshire on 18th September 1888 and was buried at St. Andrews, Fife after a full naval funeral at Portsmouth. He was survived by his wife Fanny Vining George and two children, Iris (born 1884) and Alexander (born 1887).

Henry 'Harry' Cook was born on 2nd June 1851 at 51 Castle Street, Edinburgh, and attended the Edinburgh Academy from 1860 to 1865. He went to Queensland, Australia in 1874, followed by Natal, South Africa in 1878. At the outbreak of the Zulu War he obtained a lieutenancy in a regiment of native cavalry, but fell ill and was invalided home. He was taken to Kirkcaldy, Fife to stay with his sister Lizzie, where he subsequently died on 19th July 1879. He is mentioned on the Warriston Memorial, erected by his parents in 1926.

Walter Cook was born on 15th November 1857 at 35 Great King Street, Edinburgh and attended the Edinburgh Academy from 1867 to 1869. He was appointed lieutenant in the Indian staff corps on

10th September 1875, and served through the first campaign of the Second Afghan War with the Khyber Field Force, being present at the capture of Ali Musjid and the forcing of Sissobai Pass. In the second campaign, he served as quartermaster and took part in the defence of the Shutargardan Pass under Lieutenant-Colonel G. N. Money and specially distinguished himself at the latter place on 14th October 1879. On 28th February 1880, Colonel Money wrote:-

1. When forwarding my report of the action at Shutargardan of the 14th October, and bringing specially to the notice of the lieutenant-general commanding, the conduct of Lieutenant W. Cook, 3rd Sikhs, I was not aware that it was within my province to recommend an officer for the Victoria Cross.

2. Great delay has also been occasioned in obtaining a statement from Captain Waterfield, Royal Artillery, who was the only eye-witness of the acts of gallantry for which I brought Lieutenant Cook to notice, and for which I would now beg to recommend him for the Victoria Cross.

3. The circumstances, which I hope may be considered to justify my recommendations, were as follows: the enemy occupied an excessively strong position on a rocky ridge, on the edge of which they had thrown up breastworks. The approach was difficult and almost precipitous, affording scarcely any cover. A combined attack was made upon them by three companies, 21st Punjab Native Infantry on the left, and two companies 3rd Sikhs on the right – the latter under the command of Captain Waterfield, who was serving as a volunteer – with whom was Lieutenant Cook.

Captain Waterfield and Lieutenant Cook, with a few men, had got up to within 120 yards of the crest. Here a check occurred, and Captain Waterfield said to Lieutenant Cook that it was impossible to make a final charge unless a simultaneous charge was made by the 21st, and Cook ran across under a heavy fire. He had to go about 200 yards, and returned the same way; just after his return, Captain Waterfield was shot through the thigh. Lieutenant Cook again went off, under a heavy fire, to bring up a dooly. Having given the order, he returned to his post, and when, shortly afterwards, the enemy's position was carried, he led his men in the most gallant way.

4. Lieutenant Cook's action in taking the message to the 21st was purely voluntary, as a written message could have been sent by one of the men; but he thought he would be able to explain the situation better himself. During the time passing to and from, he was never more, often less, than 120 yards from the enemy, who kept up a heavy fire on him. When afterwards going for a dooly for Captain Waterfield, although going to the rear 200 yards under heavy fire, both going and returning.

The recommendation, however, was not upheld, though Cook's gallantry was officially recorded by the adjutant-general in India. After the Shutargardan Pass was abandoned on the 30th October, he was reunited with his brother Major John Cook, VC, at Kabul, and on 10th December both brothers marched out with their respective regiments in Brigadier-General Macpherson's brigade to a camp on the Arghandi road, seven miles from the Sherpur cantonment. On 10th December, Walter Cook was involved in the fight at Surkh Kotal, and next day distinguished himself in the rear guard action under Major Griffiths, 3rd Sikhs, by which the brigade's baggage was saved. During this action, Lieutenant Walter Cook was severely wounded in the chest by an Enfield bullet, and Major John Cook, VC, of the 5th Gurkhas, was stunned by a blow to the head.

Major John Cook was wounded again on the Takht-i-Shah Peak on the 12th, and later succumbed to the wound at Sherpur. Many years later Walter Cook recalled, "I had been wounded on the 11th, in a rear guard action, covering General Macpherson's brigade, in close company with John, and indeed under his immediate command. After the action, on meeting Dr. Maloney, of the 3rd Sikhs, who diagnosed a gunshot wound affecting the left lung, I was ordered into a stretcher, and with a guard of four Sikhs, was carried to Sherpur through the city. Later, on learning that John's wound had taken a bad turn, I had myself carried down to the field hospital on several occasions to see him and was with him when he died".

On 24th February 1880, Walter Cook, having recovered from his wound, was appointed officiating adjutant with effect from 12th December 1879, but on a further reshuffle, on 12th March, he was appointed wing officer, *vice* Major Aislabie. He participated in the march from Kabul to Kandahar, and fought in the Battle of Kandahar on 1st September 1880, where his horse was wounded during the defeat of Ayub Khan. In October and November he served in the Marri Expedition as adjutant. Promoted captain on 10th September 1886, he was appointed commandant in January 1887 of a specially raised military police battalion for service in Upper Burma. Cook was appointed deputy inspector-general of military police for Burma in 1891. He became the commandant of the 30th Native Infantry in February 1892 and was advanced to the rank of major in September 1895 and lieutenant-colonel in May 1898.

During his service he was awarded the Afghanistan War Medal 1878-1880, the Kabul to Kandahar Star and the India General Service Medal 1854-1895.

Walter Cook married Mary Cunliffe Simson on 16th June 1890 at St. Gatiene, St. Andrews, her parents being Henry Bruce Simson of Brunton, Indian Civil Service (retired) and Marjory Vincent. Mary died on 3rd September 1935 at Brunton, Markinch, Fife and Walter died on 2nd April 1948 at 25 Belgrave Crescent, Edinburgh.

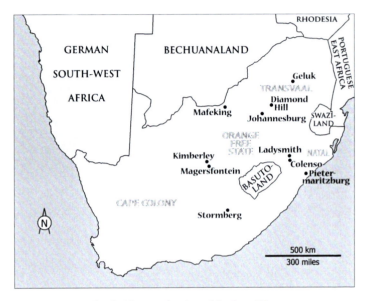

South Africa at the time of the Boer Wars
with some of the places mentioned in the text

THE SECOND BOER WAR 1899-1902

Campaign Background

The Second Boer War, generally known as the Boer War, was fought at the turn of the twentieth century, between the British Empire and the two independent Boer republics – the Orange Free State and the South African Republic (the Transvaal). After a long and hard-fought campaign, the two republics were defeated and were absorbed into the British Empire.

After the discovery of gold in the Transvaal, thousands of British and other prospectors streamed over the border from Cape Colony, as well as further afield. Johannesburg sprang up and there were tensions between the newcomers and locals. War was declared on 11th October 1899, with the Boers striking first by invading Cape Colony and Natal Colony. In December 1899, the British forces led by General Redvers Buller suffered devastating losses at Magersfontein, Stormberg and Colenso. The Boers also besieged the towns of Ladysmith, Mafeking and Kimberley.

There were further defeats for the British in early 1900 but when reinforcements arrived on 14th February, troops under the command of Field Marshall Lord Roberts launched a series of successful counter-offensives. Kimberley was relieved the next day and there were further victories before the relief of Ladysmith. However, it was the relief of Mafeking in May that prompted the biggest celebrations in Britain. As 250,000 British troops, under the overall command of Lord Kitchener, gained control of both republics, the enemy resorted to guerrilla tactics. The war rumbled on until the Boers finally conceded defeat in 1902.

6.

EDWARD DOUGLAS BROWN, VC, CB
(later BROWNE-SYNGE-HUTCHISON)
(EA 1870-1871)

born on 6th March 1861 in India

died on 3rd February 1940 in London

Citation

The award of the Victoria Cross, for action at Geluk, Eastern Transvaal, South Africa on 13th October 1900, was published on p. 308 of *London Gazette* No. 27266, dated 15th January 1901.

> *14th Hussars... Major E. D. Brown*
>
> **On 13th October 1900, at Geluk, when the enemy were within 400 yards, and bringing a heavy fire to bear, Major Brown, seeing that Sergeants Hersey's horse was shot, stopped behind the last squadron as it was retiring, and helped Sergeant Hersey to mount behind him, carrying him for about three-quarters of a mile to a place of safety. He did this under heavy fire. Major Brown afterwards enabled Lieutenant Browne, 14th Hussars, to mount, by holding his horse, which was very restive under heavy fire. Lieutenant Browne could not otherwise have mounted. Subsequently Major Brown carried Lance Corporal Trumpeter Leigh out of the action.**

He was decorated with the VC by HRH the Duke of Cornwall & York (the future King George V) at a parade in Pietermaritzburg, Natal, South Africa, on 14th August 1901. Edward's medals are held at the 14th/20th King's Hussar Museum at Stanley Street, Preston, Lancashire.

Edward Douglas Brown was born on 6th March 1861 at Kussonlie, Dagshai, India. His parents were Major David Philip Brown, 7th (Queen's Own) Hussars, and Frances Dorothy Synge-Hutchison. Edward attended the Edinburgh Academy from 1870-1871 in class 1, before going to Windermere College, Cumberland, and later, the United Services College at Westward Ho, Somerset.

Service Career

Edward was originally in the Irish Militia, but was gazetted lieutenant to the 18th Hussars on 7th November 1883, and promoted captain on 8th August 1888. He was transferred to the 14th Hussars on 27th March 1889 and was appointed commandant of the School of Instruction for Yeomanry and Volunteer Cavalry, at Aldershot,

Hampshire, from 1st January to 31st December 1894.

He was promoted major on 28th January 1899 and went to South Africa, where he took part in the Second Boer War between 1899 and 1902, winning his VC at Geluk, Eastern Transvaal for saving the lives of three men, one after the other, all of whom had been wounded during the action.

He was present at the Battle of Diamond Hill and received a mention in despatches. He was given the brevet of lieutenant-colonel on 17th June 1902 (back-dated to 29th November 1900) and assumed command of the 14th Hussars for the last seven months of the war. He was mentioned in Lord Roberts and Lord Kitchener's despatches, and given the brevet of colonel on 29th November 1906. He was promoted lieutenant-colonel on 22nd February 1907 and colonel on 22nd February 1911. Finally, he was appointed colonel commandant of the 14th /20th Hussars.

Post Military Life

He was created a CB (Military Division) in the King's birthday honours list on p. 5326 of *London Gazette* No. 29180, dated 3rd June 1915. He was also created Knight of Grace and Knight of Justice of the Order of St. John of Jerusalem, and was a member of the Ambulance Committee of the Order from 1911 to 1921. He became a Freeman and Liveryman of the Worshipful Company of Spectacle Makers of the City of London and Freeman of the City of London in 1911. In 1904, he assumed, by Royal Licence, his mother's maiden name and became Browne-Synge-Hutchinson.

Death

He died at his home at 833 Mount Royal, Marble Arch, London on 3rd February 1940, was cremated at Golders Green crematorium, northwest London on 7th March 1940, and his ashes were scattered on the disposal lawns there.

Memorials

Edward is commemorated on the European Bengal Fusilier Memorial at Winchester Cathedral, Hampshire and his name is on the VC Roll of Honour at the Union Jack Club, Sandell Street, Waterloo, London.

The Victoria Cross and George Cross memorial stone in Westminster Abbey, London

*The Western Front of World War I
with some of the places mentioned in the text*

THE FIRST WORLD WAR 1914-1918

Campaign Background

The First Battle of Ypres

Early in the war, in support of the principle of Belgian neutrality, British forces crossed the Channel, and at Mons in Belgium the British Expeditionary Force (BEF) was in action. Later that year the Battle for Flanders centred on Ypres. The BEF took and held it early in October, and on 15th October, when the first heavy German attack was launched on the town, Ypres entered British history. It was during the First Battle of Ypres that Walter Lorrain Brodie (EA 1892-1899) was in the action for which he was awarded the Victoria Cross.

The Battle of the Somme

On 21st March 1918, German artillery opened a gas and high-explosive bombardment along the front from the Scarpe River (Arras) to the Oise River (La Fère) 100 miles to the south-east. It is believed that the attack was planned to split the French and British armies and capture Amiens. From 22nd March, the Allies were driven back and by 5th April the forward troops were within 10 miles of Amiens. Though this was undeniably a setback for the Allies, they could be thankful that at least Amiens had not been taken, and nor had the French and British armies been split. It was during the early part of the battle that Allan Ebenezer Ker (EA 1890-1899) was in the action for which he was awarded the Victoria Cross.

7.

WALTER LORRAIN BRODIE, VC, MC
(EA 1892-1899)

born on 28th July 1884 in Edinburgh
died on 21st August 1918 at the Battle of Albert, France

Citation

The award of the Victoria Cross, for action at Becelaere, Belgium, on 11th November 1914, was published on p. 10661 of *London Gazette* No. 29005, dated 12th December 1914.

> His Majesty the King has been graciously pleased to approve the grant of the Victoria Cross to Lieutenant Walter Lorrain Brodie, 2nd Battalion, the Highland Light Infantry, for conspicuous bravery whilst serving with the Expeditionary Force, as set forth below:-
>
> For conspicuous gallantry near Becelaere on the 11th November, in clearing the enemy out of a portion of our trenches which they had succeeded in occupying. Heading the charge, he bayoneted several of the enemy, and thereby relieved a dangerous situation. As a result of Lieutenant Brodie's promptitude, 80 of the enemy were killed, and 51 taken prisoners.

Walter was decorated with the Victoria Cross by HM King George V at Windsor Castle on 12th December 1914. His medal is not publicly held.

Walter Lorrain Brodie was born on 28th July 1884 at 13 Belgrave Place, Edinburgh, third child of four (two sons and two daughters) of John Brodie, chartered accountant, and Grace Mary Lorrain. Walter attended the Edinburgh Academy from 1892-1899 in classes P1 to 'special'. In the 1901 census, Walter (aged 15) is described as a student, and is living at 23 Belgrave Crescent, Edinburgh, with his mother, brother Patrick (20), sisters Grace (19) and Mary (5) and three servants. Patrick Brodie, Walter's brother, attended the Academy from 1889-1898.

Service Career

Walter Lorrain Brodie was commissioned into the Highland Light Infantry in March 1904, joined the 2nd Battalion in Jersey, Channel Islands, and was then stationed at the Castle, Edinburgh and Fort George, Inverness-shire. He was promoted to lieutenant on 30th June 1908 and was stationed at Cork and Mullingar, Ireland between

1909 and 1913.

Walter sailed for France as the battalion machine-gun officer on 13th August 1914 with the 2nd Division. He was promoted captain on 10th September 1914 and took part in action at Ypres, Belgium. For his gallantry in action at Becelaere, Belgium on 11th November 1914, he was awarded the Victoria Cross as described in the citation above.

He took part in the fighting at Richebourg, Givenchy and Festubert in 1915, and was attached for intelligence duties to the staff to Sir Hubert Gough and later to Sir Henry Rawlinson. He was appointed brigade major of 63rd Infantry Brigade in May 1916 and took part in the Battle of the Somme and of Arras in 1916. He was awarded the Military Cross in January 1917.

Walter assumed command of the 2nd /10th Liverpool Scottish Battalion at the end of 1917 and was given the brevet of major in January 1918. He was appointed commanding officer of the 2nd Battalion, Highland Light Infantry in April 1918 and took part in the Battle of Albert, which began on 21st August 1918 and in which he was killed in action.

Burial

Walter was buried at Bienvillers Military Cemetery, Pas de Calais, France, plot XVIII F. 15.

Memorial

His name is on the VC Roll of Honour at the Union Jack Club, Sandell Street, Waterloo, London. His name is also recorded on the War Memorial at the Edinburgh Academy.

*The Victoria Cross and George Cross memorial stone
in Westminster Abbey, London, with wreaths laid on 26th June 2006*

8.

ALLAN EBENEZER KER, VC
(EA 1890-1899)

born on 5th March 1883 in Edinburgh

died on 12th September 1958 in Hampstead, London

Citation

The award of the Victoria Cross, for action at St. Quentin, France on 21st March 1918, was published on p. 11205 of the *London Gazette* No. 31536, dated 4th September 1919.

Lieutenant Allan Ebenezer Ker, 3rd Battalion, Gordon Highlanders, attached 61st Battalion, Machine Corps.

For most conspicuous bravery and devotion to duty – on the 21st March, 1918, near St. Quentin, France, after a heavy bombardment, the enemy penetrated our line, and the flank of the 61st Division became exposed. Lieutenant Ker with one Vickers gun succeeded in engaging the enemy's infantry, approaching under cover of dead ground, and held up the lie attack, inflicting many casualties. He then sent back word to his Battalion Headquarters that he had determined to stop with his Sergeant and several other men who had been badly wounded and fight until a counter-attack could be launched to relieve him. Just as ammunition failed, his party were attacked from behind by the enemy with bombs, machine guns, and with bayonet. Several bayonet attacks were delivered, but each time they were repulsed by Lieutenant Ker and his companions with their revolvers, the Vickers machine gun having by this time been destroyed. The wounded were collected into a small shelter, and it was decided to defend them to the last and to hold up the enemy as long as possible. In one of the many hand-to-hand encounters a German rifle and bayonet and a small supply of ammunition was secured, and subsequently used with good effect against the enemy. Although Lieutenant Ker was very exhausted from want of food and gas poisoning and from the supreme exertions he had made during ten hours of the most severe bombardment, fighting, and attending to the wounded, he refused to surrender until all his ammunition was exhausted and his position was rushed by large numbers of the enemy. His behaviour throughout the day was absolutely cool and fearless, and by his determination he was materially instrumental in engaging and holding up for three hours more than 500 of the enemy.

Allan Ker was decorated with the VC by HM King George V at Buckingham Palace on 26th November 1919. His medals are in the Ashcroft Collection.

Allan Ebenezer Ker was born on 5th March 1883 at 16 Findhorn Place, Edinburgh, first child of four (two sons, two daughters) of Robert Darling Ker, WS, and Johanna Johnston. After schooling at the Academy in classes P1 to 4b, he went to Edinburgh University and studied there from 1903 to 1908. At the time of the 1891 census, the Ker family was living at Westgrove, Ferry Road, Edinburgh, and at the time of the 1901 census they were living at 4 Wardie Road, Edinburgh. In 1901 Allan is described as being a law apprentice.

He was appointed a member of the Society of Writers to His Majesty's Signet in 1908 and was employed as an associate solicitor with his father in Edinburgh. In 1916, he married Vera Irene Gordon-Skinner at Grantham, Lincolnshire and they had two daughters, Vera G. Skinner, born 1916, and Adrienne Ann Mary Veronica Carmell Skinner, born 1920, both in Wandsworth, London.

Service Career

In about 1908, Allan joined the Queen's Edinburgh Mounted Infantry, but enlisted in the 3rd Battalion the Gordon Highlanders on 11th June 1915 as a 2nd lieutenant. Apparently Allan travelled to Aberdeen towards the end of 1914 to settle the affairs of his cousin, Captain Arthur Milford Ker, Gordon Highlanders, who had been killed in action on 14 October 1914. Allan was planning to enlist in the Royal Scots Greys, but whilst at the Gordon Highlanders barracks, he was persuaded to join the famous Highland regiment.

He went to France in October 1915, and was attached to the Machine Corps in March 1916. From there he went to Salonica about July 1916 and took part in the Battle of Muchovo near the Vardar River (see map on p. 60). He was evacuated from Salonica to the UK with malignant malaria in December 1916.

Allan was promoted lieutenant on 1st January 1917 and returned to the Western Front on 15th May 1917, taking part in the fighting at Passchendale, Arras, Ypres, Cambrai and eventually at St.Quentin, which was where he took part in the action for which he was awarded the Victoria Cross.

He was taken prisoner on 21st March 1918 and held at Karlsruhe until July 1918, then in Beeskow in der Mark. Whilst in captivity he was the secretary and food controller for British officers in both lagers. He was repatriated on 16th December 1918.

After the war, he remained a Gordon Highlander, attached

to the Machine Corps, but was specially employed in the Judge Advocate General's department in Cologne, Germany in 1919. Having returned to England, he became a temporary captain at the War Office on 1st April 1920, having been appointed staff captain on 1st March 1920, an appointment he held until 31st March 1922. He was promoted captain on 1st January 1921, appointed to a specialist employment with the Gordon Highlanders and was demobilised on 23rd May 1922 and transferred to the reserve.

Allan was recalled to the Colours on 29th October 1940, serving in the directorate of the chief of the imperial staff at the War Office as a general staff officer grade 2. He attended the Potsdam Conference. He was awarded Knight of the Order of Military Merit (Brazil) in 1944.

Post Military Life

Allan was a partner in Clarke, Rawlins, Ker & Co. Solicitors in Calcutta, India. He returned to England in 1946 and found employment with the rents tribunal for Paddington and Marylebone, London. He was also chairman of the Fifth Army Comrades Association.

Unknown Warrior – VC Guard of Honour

On 11th November 1920, the body of an unknown warrior from the Great War was interred near the Great West Door of Westminster Abbey, and a guard of honour was mounted by members of Britain's highest order of courage. Lieutenant Allan Ker was present as a member of that guard of honour.

He also attended the unveiling of the Machine Gun Corps Memorial at Hyde Park Corner on 10th May 1926.

Death

Allan Ker died on 12th September 1958 at New Garden Hospital, Hampstead, London and was buried in West Hampstead Cemetery, Fortune Green Road, Hampstead, London on 17th September 1958.

Memorial

His name is on the VC Roll of Honour at the Union Jack Club, Sandell Street, Waterloo, London.

The eastern Mediterranean Sea
with some of the places mentioned in the text

THE SECOND WORLD WAR 1939-1945

Campaign Background

The Mediterranean Sea

In 1940, Italy had failed in its attempt to overrun Greece, but the following year Germany invaded the country. In 1941, Britain moved troops to defend Crete, with final reinforcements arriving just four days before the start of the German invasion of the strategically important island. Meanwhile the British Army was facing Field Marshall Rommel in North Africa, so the eastern Mediterranean Sea was a very active area of conflict.

9.

ANTHONY CECIL CAPEL MIERS, VC, KBE, CB, DSO & Bar
(EA 1915-1916)

born on 11th November 1806 in Inverness

died on 30th June 1985 at Roehampton, Surrey

Citation

The award of the Victoria Cross, for action at Corfu harbour, Ionian Sea, on 4th March 1942, was published on p. 2983 of *London Gazette* No. 35622, dated 7th July 1942. The citation read:

> *Commander Anthony Cecil Capel Miers DSO, Royal Navy.*
>
> **For valour in command of H.M. Submarine Torbay in a daring and successful raid on shipping in a defended enemy harbour, planned with full knowledge of the great hazards to be expected during seventeen hours in waters closely patrolled by the enemy. On arriving in the harbour he had to charge his batteries lying on the surface in full moonlight, under the guns of the enemy. As he could not see his target he waited several hours and attacked in full daylight in a glassy calm. When he had fired his torpedoes he was heavily counter-attacked and had to withdraw through a long channel with anti-submarine craft all round and continuous air patrols overhead.**

He was decorated with the VC by HM King George VI at Buckingham Palace on 28th July 1942. Anthony Miers's VC and medals, donated by Lady Miers, are currently held and displayed at the Imperial War Museum, Lambeth Road, London.

Anthony Cecil Capel Miers was born at Birchwood, Inverness, on 11th November 1906, the third child of six (four sons and two daughters) of Douglas Nathaniel Carelton Capel Miers, captain and adjutant Cameron Highlanders, and Margaret Annie Christie. Anthony was educated at Stubbington House School, Fareham, Hampshire and attended the Academy in the year 1915-1916 in class P5b, after which he was at Wellington College, Crowthorne, Berkshire.

Anthony's father, Douglas Miers, born in 1875, served in the 3rd Battalion, Queen's Own Cameron Highlanders, in the rank of captain and saw action in the Nile Expedition in 1895. He served in the Second Boer War and was present during operations in Cape Colony, Orange Free State, the Transvaal, Orange River Colony, Wittebergen and Ladybrand from October 1899 to September 1900.

He was mentioned in despatches on 10th September 1901 and was awarded the Royal Humane Society's Bronze Medal for saving the life of Lieutenant Maturan, Royal Artillery from the Vaal River, South Africa, in 1900. He was adjutant of the regiment in 1906, serving at Cameron Barracks at Inverness and also served in the Great War with the 1st Battalion, Cameron Highlanders. He was killed in action in France on 25th September 1914 and buried at Bourg-et-Comin Communal Cemetery, Aisne, France.

Naval Career

Anthony joined the Royal Navy as a special entry cadet in 1924 aboard *HMS Thunderer*. He was promoted midshipman on 15th September 1925 and to sub-lieutenant on 1st January 1928. He joined the Submarine Service on 24th April 1929 aboard *HMS Dolphin*, carrying out training to August 1929. He was promoted lieutenant on 1st January 1930.

Anthony was appointed to *HM Submarine M-2*, the giant submarine-monitor, as part of the 5th Submarine Flotilla at Portsmouth in 1931 and then as first officer aboard *HM Submarine H-28* at Harwich, Essex.

It is reported that he threatened to strike a rating in the heat of the moment during a football match in 1933. The matter was soon common knowledge on board, but would have rested there had not Miers himself voluntarily reported it. He was subsequently court-martialled and dismissed from his ship.

Anthony was appointed first lieutenant aboard *HM Submarine Rainbow* in 1933 in the Far East. He attended and passed the 'periscope' course for submarine captains in 1936, and assumed command of *HM Submarine L-54* on 8th August 1936, which he commanded at the 1937 coronation review at the Spithead. He was appointed to the training ship *HMS Iron Duke* at Portsmouth on 1st October 1937 and was promoted lieutenant-commander on 1st January 1938, attending and passing Staff College in 1938.

He was appointed to the sea-going staff of the Commander-in-Chief Home Fleet (Admiral of the Fleet Sir Charles Forbes) in 1939 aboard *HMS Nelson*, *HMS Rodney* and *HMS Warspite*. He was mentioned in despatches in 1940 and again on 1st January 1941 and he was awarded a Distinguished Service Order and Bar for sinking or damaging over 70,000 tons of Axis shipping.

Command of HM Submarine Torbay

Anthony assumed command of the newly built (1st April 1940) T-class submarine *HMS Torbay* on 12th November 1940. *HMS Torbay* sailed from Chatham, Kent in January 1941 for sea trials and then sailed for patrol at Alexandria, Egypt on 22nd April 1941, arriving around 13th May 1941. About a year later the *Torbay* returned to the UK for a re-fit, but in the intervening year under the command of Miers, she carried out numerous patrols in the eastern Mediterranean Sea. Most of these patrols were in the nature of general attacks on enemy shipping, but four are worth describing in some detail.

Third Patrol – The Aegean Sea – 28th June to 15th July 1941

The first action was the sinking of a caique off Falkonera on 30th June. They later sank the merchant ship, *Citta di Tripoli*, on 2nd July, followed by a caique and a schooner, both flying the swastika and carrying troops. All troops were killed by gunfire. Sank the Italian submarine *Jantina* off the island of Mykoni on 5th July 1941.

While sailing westwards to the Kythera Channel to the north-west of Crete on 8th July Miers destroyed a swastika-flying schooner. He then took part in what the company later labelled 'the battle of the caiques' on the following day. Four caiques and a schooner carrying German troops with British ammunition, petrol and food supplies were sighted between the isles of Kythera and Antikythera, sailing from Crete towards Cape Malea in the Peloponnese. As soon as the *Torbay* surfaced, the convoy scattered and made to escape towards Antikythera. It is believed that the troops on board were probably German 11th Air Corps who had conquered Crete and had now been relieved by garrison troops. *Torbay* fired on the vessels and only one subsequently escaped. In one case a caique hailed *Torbay* – "Captain is Greek; we surrender." Miers's crew formed the opinion that the voice did not sound Greek. The *Torbay* pulled alongside when Corporal Bremner, of the London Scottish (Gordon Highlanders) from the Folbot (Folded Boat) Section of No 8 Commando, embarked to carry out special operations, spotted one of the crew in the act of throwing a grenade and promptly shot him. Lieutenant Paul Campbell, the second-in-command, who was standing on the casing ready to board the caique, saw a German pointing a rifle at him from behind the wheelhouse, so he promptly shot him. What happened next was openly covered in Miers's logbook of the patrol dated 9th July 1941 – that having boarded the small German-flagged freighter and laid demolition charges, '…submarine cast off and with the Lewis gun accounted for the soldiers in the rubber raft…'

With the dawning of a new day, several aircraft were spotted searching the area, so the crew formed the opinion that the action must have been observed from the shore, which was fairly close.

Fourth Patrol – Gulf of Sirte and Crete – 2nd to 28th August 1941

The main function of the fourth patrol was to recover a Special Service officer, Lieutenant-Commander Pool RNR, who had landed in Crete the previous month on a special mission. His mission had been to make contact with resistance elements on the island and to deliver stores and certain instructions. He had also directed friendly elements to the Preveli Monastery in south-western Crete to await evacuation.

Torbay positioned herself north-west of Paximadia Island off the south-west part of Crete on 18th August under hazardous conditions. A force eight gale was blowing from the north and the daylight hours were spent reconnoitring the beach through the periscope for Bremner's benefit, as his was the task of conducting the journeys from *Torbay* to the shore and back using the folbot.

Lieutenant-Commander Pool contacted the *Torbay* from the shore at 2100 hrs using the prearranged signal. Miers directed Bremner to set sail, but Bremner explained that the conditions were too dangerous. A heated argument broke out between the two men but Miers concluded by giving Bremner a direct order, at which point the folbot was launched.

A few moments later Miers had second thoughts and gave orders for the collection of Bremner before he drowned. *Torbay* pursued and recovered Bremner before moving in closer to shore. Bremner eventually landed at about 2300 hrs, but was unable to locate Pool as he had vacated the area some 30 minutes previously. Bremner was able to ferry an Australian sergeant and a New Zealand soldier to the *Torbay* with information that there were many stranded Commonwealth troops in the vicinity. Whilst ashore, Bremner had made contact with Cretans giving instructions that he would probably return the following night to collect authorised personnel for subsequent transport to Egypt and safety.

Bremner volunteered to ferry personnel from the shore to *Torbay* over a period of three consecutive nights, which, given the danger of such repeated activity in the same location, was extremely hazardous. Fortunately the Germans never spotted her during the evacuations, and, in all, 13 officers and 117 other ranks were evacuated, plus Lieutenant-Commander Pool and his party.

For his devotion to duty on this and other occasions Bremner was awarded the Military Medal and Lieutenant-Commander Pool was awarded the Distinguished Service Order.

Sixth and Seventh Patrols – Gulf of Sirte, Beda Littoria – 7th to 18th October and 10th to 24th November 1941

Miers was ordered to take part in a special operation with *HM Submarine Talisman* to land Scottish commandos behind Rommel's lines to create havoc to command and control at a date to coincide with the opening of General Sir Alan Cunningham's Western Desert offensive known as 'Operation Crusader'. It was also hoped to kill General Rommel, the leader of the German Afrika Corps.

Lieutenant-Colonel Geoffrey Keyes, MC, hatched the plan to eliminate Rommel using a Commando force, based on intelligence gathered by Captain Jock Haseldon of the Libyan Arab Force, who had virtually been living as an Arab in the desert. Keyes selected himself to command the operation, code-named 'Flipper', and boarded the submarine *Torbay* at Alexandria, Egypt, on 10th November 1941 with a force of two officers and 22 commandos. Lieutenant-Colonel Robert Laycock (later General Sir Robert Laycock), with a force of two officers and 24 commandos, boarded *Talisman* at the same time and they landed on a beach at Chessem-el-Chelb four days later. Waiting on the beach were Captain Haseldon and an Arab soldier from G(R) Branch to guide the folbots and dinghies to the beach and to assist in bringing the vessels ashore. The remainder of Haseldon's men, comprising two British officers, a Free Belgian captain and an Arab soldier, were laid up inland. All had been dropped in the area earlier in the day by the Long Range Desert Group.

Haseldon flashed his torch out to sea at 1830 hrs and by 1859 hrs the first of the folbots arrived out of the darkness. However, before all the men could disembark from the submarines, heavy seas intervened and only seven men and Laycock himself made it ashore from the *Talisman*. There was now an immediate need to review the plans, taking into account the reduced resources and overriding need to co-ordinate the raids with Operation Crusader. On the night of the 18th, amended plans were drawn up as follows: an attack on Rommel's house and HQ by Keyes and 18 other ranks, the sabotage of telephone and telegraph communications at the cross-road of Cyrene by Lieutenant Cook and 6 other ranks and on the El Frida to Slonta road by Haseldon and his 5 other ranks. Under cover of darkness on the 15th they set off on their 15 to 20 mile trek in heavy rain. Keyes would be awarded a posthumous VC for his part in the unsuccessful raid. Of the attacking force, only Laycock, Haseldon and Sergeant Jack Terry escaped death or capture and made it back to Cairo.

Tenth Patrol – various locations including Corfu – 20th February to 18th March 1942

Miers attempted to attack a Cortatone-class destroyer in the late afternoon of the 3rd March, but was spotted. The destroyer came with a pattern of six depth-charges which exploded in close proximity to the submarine, lifting her some five feet. He moved his patrol to Corfu Island where he sighted a large enemy convoy escorted by three destroyers entering Corfu harbour on 3rd March. Miers followed the convoy at slow speed until dusk, when he surfaced and entered the southern channel. He had to dive again to avoid a small motor ship but then surfaced and followed it in.

At 2200 hrs he recharged his batteries about five miles east of the main anchorage, where he waited until daylight. By this time the convoy had apparently sailed again, but there were two 5,000 ton transports and a destroyer still in the anchorage. He was able to sink the two transports, but missed the destroyer. The *Torbay* was again depth-charged forty times while making its escape to the open sea, after being in closely patrolled enemy waters for seventeen hours.

For his gallantry during the eighth, ninth and tenth patrols, and particularly for his action at Corfu, he was awarded the Victoria Cross.

Other Awards

In respect of their operations on the *Torbay* during their spell of duty in the eastern Mediterranean, the following awards (apart from Miers's VC) were made to personnel:

two Distinguished Service Crosses
thirteen Distinguished Service Medals

one Companion of the Distinguished Service Order
two Bars to the Distinguished Service Cross
four Bars to the Distinguished Service Medal
eight mentioned in despatches

Anthony Miers subsequent Naval Career

Miers was appointed submarine liaison officer to the staff of Admiral
Chester William Nimitz, C-in-C US Pacific Fleet at Pearl Harbour,
Hawaii, and of Commander Submarines Pacific, Admiral Lockwood,
in December 1942. He took part in a 56-day war patrol with the
US Submarine Cabrilla, assumed command of the 8th Submarine
Flotilla, aboard *HMS Maidstone* at Perth, Australia in 1944 and
assumed command of *HMS Vernon II* during the Ramillies and
Malaya Campaign in 1946.

Miers was promoted captain on 31st December 1946, and
attended and passed the Joint Services Staff College in 1947. He
gained his 'A' pilot's licence in 1948 and later that year he assumed
command of *HMS Blackcap*, the Royal Naval Air Station at Stretton,
Cheshire, and in 1950, command of *HMS Forth* and the 1st
Submarine Flotilla Mediterranean Fleet. He was appointed to and
later made captain of the Royal Naval College at Greenwich, London,
in 1952. In 1954 he assumed command of the aircraft carrier *HMS
Theseus*, was promoted rear admiral on 7th January 1956 and was
appointed Flag Officer, Middle East that same year. He retired from
the Royal Navy on 4th August 1959.

Miscellaneous

One of his training officers early in his career wrote that Miers
would either be awarded the VC or a Court Martial – in the event
he achieved both!

He was described as totally loyal, outstandingly keen, fearless,
hot-tempered and incautiously outspoken. He became known as
'Gamp' on the lower deck and as 'Crap' by officers, for reasons that
have never been convincingly explained. He was fiercely competitive
at sea, ashore and on the playing field and was a good athlete, a tennis
and squash player, and a fine rugby footballer. He played rugby
for the London Scottish, Combined Services and Hampshire and
was selected for trials for the Navy and for Scotland. His vigorous
single-minded aim at all times was to overcome all obstacles in

war. The men who served him had complete confidence in him and forgave his impetuous outbursts. Nobody could be indifferent to his presence. One of his ship's company, Leading Stoker Philip Le Gros, once remarked, "the thing about the commander was that he would get us into trouble but he always got us out of it."

Marriage and Family

Anthony Miers married Patricia Mary Millar of the Women's Royal Australia Naval Service at Perth, Australia on 20th January 1945. They had a daughter, Angela Miers, and a son, John A. C. Miers.

Post Service Career and Life

He was a director of Francis Sumner (1959-1962), chairman and managing director of Buttons Ltd. (1959-1963), worked for Mills & Allen Ltd. (1962-1974), and the London & Provincial Poster Group (1962-1971). He was later a consultant there (1971-1983), director for the Development Co-ordination of National Car Parks (1971) and chairman of Hudsons Offshore Ltd. (1972-1973).

He was a president of various naval sports associations and member of numerous clubs or societies including, amongst many, the MCC, London Scottish Rugby Football Club and the Royal Highland Society.

He was Under Warden of the Worshipful Company of Tin Plate Workers in 1982 and later Upper Warden (1983) and Master (1984). The Worshipful Company was established by Royal Charter about 1670. One of his forbears, Nathaniel Miers of Swansea and Neath, was an original member of that Livery Company and its Master in 1712. Since then there has always been a Miers, several having been Masters, on the Court.

Freedom of the Burgh of Inverness

For the second time in history, a triple freedom ceremony took place in Inverness on 14th April 1955, the first time being in 1930. On this occasion the three men were 'the Rt. Hon. Thomas Johnston, CH, Chairman of the North of Scotland Hydro Electric Board and a former outstanding Secretary of State for Scotland; Sir Hugh Mackenzie, CBE, Deputy Chairman of the Hydro Electric Board, who was Provost of Inverness from 1934 to 1945; and Captain Anthony C. C. Miers, VC, DSO, RN, a native of Inverness, who had received the supreme award for valour when he was a submarine commander in 1942. He was also appointed a Freeman of the City of London in 1966'.

Other Citations

He was appointed a Companion of the Distinguished Service Order (DSO) in 1941 for 'courage, enterprise and devotion to duty in successful submarine patrols'; awarded a Bar to his DSO in 1942, for 'courage, skill and coolness in successful submarine patrols'; appointed to the degree of officer of the Legion of Merit (USA), bestowed by the President of the United States of America in 1946, 'for distinguished service to the Allied cause throughout the war'; and appointed a Companion of the Military Division of the Order of the Bath (CB) in 1958; and made a KBE on 13th June 1959.

Death

Anthony Cecil Capel Miers died at his home at 8 Highdown Road, Roehampton, Surrey on 30th June 1985. He was buried in the Roman Catholic Section of the Tomnahurich Cemetery, Inverness, where there is a memorial to him.

A memorial service was held in the Cathedral of St. George, Southwark in 1985. HRH The Duke of Edinburgh was represented by Admiral of the Fleet Sir John Fieldhouse, Chief of the Defence Staff and a submariner. The Board of the Admiralty were also there.

Memorial

There is a memorial to him in Tomnahurich Cemetery, as just stated, and his name is on the VC Roll of Honour at the Union Jack Club, Sandell Street, Waterloo, London.

Selected references and reading

Books

The Thin Red Line: War, Empire and Visions of Scotland, by Stuart Allan & Allan Carswell; NMS Enterprises: Publishing, Edinburgh, 2004. ISBN 1-901-66387-6.

Symbol of Courage - a complete history of the Victoria Cross, by Max Arthur; Sidgwick & Jackson, London 2004. ISBN 0-283-07351-9.

Victoria Cross Heroes: Men of Valour, by Michael Ashcroft; Headline Book Publishing, London, 2006. ISBN 0-755-31632-0.

The Freemen of Inverness, by W. J. Mackay; The Highland Herald Ltd., Inverness, 1975.

The Clacken and the Slate, by Magnus Magnusson; Collins, London, 1974. ISBN 0-004-11170-2.

175 Accies, by Bill Stirling; the Edinburgh Academy, 1999.

Web sites

History of the Victoria Cross
www.victoriacross.org.uk

East India Company VCs
www.haileybury.herts.sch.uk/archives/roll/heic vc.htm